Nets in the Wind

Alastair Ashford-Brown

Also Available from Bardic Press

New Nightingale, New Rose:
Poems From the Divan of Hafiz
translated by Richard Le Gallienne

The Door of the Beloved: Poems of Hafiz
translated by Justin McCarthy

The Quatrains of Omar Khayyam:
Three Translations of the Rubaiyat
*translated by Edward Fitzgerald, Justin McCarthy
and Richard Le gallienne*

The Four Branches of the Mabinogi:
Celtic Myth and Medieval Reality
Will Parker

Visit our website at www.bardic-press.com
email us at info@bardic-press.com

Nets in the Wind

Alastair Ashford-Brown

Bardic Press
Cadoxton/Tregatwg 2019

Nets in the Wind
Copyright © 2019 A.M. Ashford-Brown

Printed on acid-free paper

Published by Bardic Press
Wesley House
Cadoxton
Barry
Vale of Glamorgan
CF63 1JY
Wales

http://www.bardic-press.com
info@bardic-press.com

Cover painting by A.M. Ashford-Brown

CONTENTS

SPRING WINDS	1
I HARDLY KNOW IF I'M STILL I	2
PROVINCIAL TOWN IN THE RAIN	3
THE SINGING BRIDGE	4
THE TALE UNFOLDING FOR YOU AND ME.	5
UNSPEAKABLE EVENING	6
FOR MARINA TSVETAEVA	7
ON A PAINTING BY CHAGALL	8
TAMARA	9
THE MOUTH FROM WHICH SUCH SWEET SONGS CAME	10
I THINK I'LL STAY IN TODAY	11
THESE GIRLS WITH THEIR PARASOLS	12
AT THE TAXI RANK WITH YOU	13
ON READING 'SORROW', BY THE POETESS CHU SHU CHEN	14
MY SECRET ME	15
BLOSSOMS ON THE CHERRY TREE	16
AND I THOUGHT AND I TURNED AND I THOUGHT	17
AVEC SON MEC MARIE...	18
THE WANDERER SAYS GOODBYE TO HIS COAT	19
IT SLOWLY DAWNS ON ME	20
ANNETTE...	21
I KNEW A POET IN ROMANIA	22
SHE	23
WEATHER VANE	25
I CANNOT EXTRACT FROM THESE SORROWS THE PLOUGH	28
AFFAIR	29
CHANNEL CROSSING	30
YOU CANNOT QUITE CATCH HER EYE	31
ONLY THE DEVIL KNEW	32

THESE POEMS WHICH FESTER IN THE DARKNESS	33
FULL YOUTH AND BLEEDING	34
I CAN CHANGE THE FORTUNES OF MEN	35
NOW IT'S SPRING, LOOK AROUND!	37
SHE WINKS HER EYE AT HIS CONUNDRUM	38
I IMAGINE LI PO	39
I CLOTHE THIS SKELETON	40
AT THE TIME OF THE BLOOD	41
MISS MERVÉ	42
MY ARITHMETIC'S NOT QUITE UP TO THAT	43
ÖZGÜR	44
PHILIP THE BALD	45
ADVICE TO THE YOUTH WHICH ONCE WAS I	46
STORM IN THE HARBOUR	47
PATMOS	48
ENGÜR	49
LOST IN THE SHADOWS I'VE THROWN AROUND MY SOUL	50
THE PHOTOGRAPH	51
THIS HAS MY HEART MOVED	52
AROUSAL	53
IT WAS LONDON THAT YOU WANTED	54
LEYLA	55
AYSEGÜL	56
CURSED AM I	57
STRAYMUM	58
TO AN UNKNOWN WOMAN PASSING	59
OUT OF MY MIND – OUT!	60
WHEN I, WITH MANY THOUGHTS IN MIND	61
THREE POEMS TO AUTUMN	63
HOMESICKNESS	65
WRECKED ON THE BALTIC	66
WINTER WALKS ALONG THE DANUBE	68

WITH SOMETHING AKIN TO HOPE	69
SHE COMES TO PICK UP HER THINGS	70
I CANNOT GO IN!	71
MY POEM	72
THE TIME HAS COME I THINK	74
THAT IS WHY I AVERT MY EYE	75
CHANTRAI	76
WAKING AWAY FROM A DREAM	77
SAPPHO	78
I WAS A YOUTH AND SADLY WANTING	79
THE REST IS A BLUR OF CRIMSON AND BLACK	80
GINA	82
THE COIN	83
YOU'D PUT ON YOUR SHOES THE WRONG WAY ROUND	85
WHERE HAVE YOU GONE?	86
THE RIVER OF TIME WHICH NEVER RETURNS	87
I TOOK HER WORDS TO MEAN WHAT SHE MEANT	89
HELÈNE...	91
HIS WAND'S ASTIR AS IT WAS BEFORE	92
NIGHT IN ISTANBUL	93
GOT YOUR LETTER, FEEL BETTER!	94

SPRING WINDS

Blossoms on the spring wind
fall into my glass
and a cheeky breeze lifts
the hem of her skirt
whilst the strings of the lute are taking me
away from the earth.

I HARDLY KNOW IF I'M STILL I

I shall try on the shoes beneath the table
see if they fit me
I shall raise a glass of beer to my lips
see if it's still to my taste
I shall call around friends
to see if they know
if the one I call I is the one who is calling

I shall re-examine my name
my passport number, photograph, date of birth
to see if anything's changed

I shall go through my memories
one by one
and see if there are some I might have forgotten

I shall ask my neighbour, the postman, my doctor
if they know who I am
I shall look in the mirror and see
if someone else is pretending he's me

And whether it's the same man
you told you loved madly
just the other day
but now when he passes
you look the other way.

PROVINCIAL TOWN IN THE RAIN

You sit in a park
and you wonder what to do –
nothing much you can do
in this provincial town
where the shops shut at five
and then the streets are empty

you could walk around in circles in the rain
be a stranger, get stared at, get wet
and end up here again

you could sidle off to a pub I suppose
and lose your blues, spend your money
but you know quite well in a sorry state
you'd end up here again –

in this little shelter in the park
staring out through the rain.

THE SINGING BRIDGE

'They come here, the little birds, to drink
vodka, and then they sing!' you said
and pointed to the ledge they alight on –
my darling drunken girl –
and then you collapsed on the steps
and laddered your stockings and cut your knee
and I gathered you up in my arms
and I sang you a happy song
just like the birds that alight on the ledge.

THE TALE UNFOLDING FOR YOU AND ME

And we drank another beer
and went on our way
over the bridges in the nights never dark
and I spun you on your heels and kissed
you over and over and over again
down by the Neva

Have you ever wondered why you and I have met
if things beyond us steer us
and this for some unknown reason's meant
though perhaps not forever ...?

We drank another beer the sky turned black
over the Baltic Sea
and the summer breeze chilled and began to tell
the tale unfolding for you and me.

UNSPEAKABLE EVENING

She took me by the hand
and her hand was full of tremoring and hurt
and mine very cold, inert

Do you remember this bridge, the Singing Bridge?
she asked, trembling as she turned to me
yes, I do, I said...
and something in my voice dismayed her –
it had not thrilled at the recollection
of when we'd kissed and she'd slipped
and laddered her stockings
and I'd sung her such a happy song –
her hand fell away from mine
I suppose she'd guessed...

What's wrong? a little irked, I asked
Nothing, take me to the metro
I want to go home.

FOR MARINA TSVETAEVA

Marina! – your very name
is that of the sea, the turbulent sea
the sea

How I have wept with you in your poems
how I have dreamt with you...!

Tender, passionate, Poet!

Your blood spills over the page
the waves your tears and your rage
ensoul these poems

My dear, what happened to you that day
with the rope and the beam
and the chair you kicked away beneath you –
or was it you?

Outside my window
the wind is troubling the trees.

ON A PAINTING BY CHAGALL

Is it Orpheus? – it seems to be
though his garb is not what one would expect
with those baggy trousers and workman's cap –
nevertheless, it seems to be him, there with his violin

A tree is waving its branches
rocks and stones are switching about
a cockerel's stepping out of the sky
a goat is hanging from a cloud, a deck of cards
or is it a fan?- spread out from its hand
whilst the moon, rocking slightly
is almost too see-through to see

Yes it's Orpheus alright
with one foot on a chair and the other
dangling in the air

TAMARA

Come any closer and I'll not be able
to hold myself back from kissing you –
alarm bells ring for I'm already demented with desire
at the smell of your skin

Ah, just what are they saying they who have seen
us locked in oblivion to all about us, existence ceased?
They have jumped to conclusions
which are entirely accurate

For I've been beyond the dictates of my will
since the moment I sank into your black eyes of Malatya
and bound in chains by your fingers
twining your hair – but Tamara I don't care
lead on at your leisure
along the twisting paths of pleasure...

THE MOUTH FROM WHICH SUCH SWEET SONGS CAME

Do you remember the busy bar in which we kissed that one
   time?
I doubt if it still exists for that was a long time ago
and so much of Athens has gone since then –
it was in Ommonia square and we were drinking beer
your guitar was hanging on the back of your chair

'You're lovely!' I said as I cupped your face in my hands
'You're not so bad yourself,' you said –
a very Scottish way of saying the same

The bar was full of smoke and steam
and the smell of souflaki which was grilling by the door
and everything was very greasy and sweaty
it was a sweltering night in August, if I rightly recall
things are a little blurred now and I forget

Everything except your lowered eyes
your breath, your mouth
sweet as the songs which came from it
when you'd stood on the street and you'd sung.

I THINK I'LL STAY IN TODAY

Today again it's pouring with rain
and there are rumbles and flashes everywhere
I fling the window wide
inhale

The hills are hidden from view
and all I can see is wind and rain
and a heron against the watery sky
visible only to a certain height
before it's swallowed in the clouds

I think I'll stay in today
and open a bottle of Chardonnay –
no point in getting wet
there are poems to be written
books to be read
and fabulous places for my mind to travel

I'll melt away in the heron's wake behind the clouds
and into the electric hills
where flashing lightning for one split second removes the
  shroud
wrapped around a world we cannot see
with a normal eye –
just as in my dreams I see it
in nature's fruits as they hang upon the bough.

THESE GIRLS WITH THEIR PARASOLS

Sweet the air
as they pass beneath the trees
slim as willows
eyes like almonds

Beyond compare
these girls of the East –
they have what makes a man stand straight
and they have what brings him to his knees

And they so utterly undo me
with their backward glances
these girls with their parasols.

AT THE TAXI RANK WITH YOU

I come back
I drink at the window
you don't realise the effect you have on me!

Past midnight
wish you were with me
we stood at a taxi rank somewhere in the suburbs
you with your violin over your shoulder
just then I'd have kissed you had I been bolder...
now I thank god that I wasn't!

For the moon was a scimitar
it hung in the night a menacing blade
like the silver crescent which swung at your ear
and the ring on your finger newly-placed there
glowered in the street lights – 'don't you dare!'

But O how your hair flowed down the sides of your neck
over your shoulders down to your breast
where my heart in its turmoil
dangled distressed!

ON READING 'SORROW', BY THE POETESS CHU SHU CHEN

Your poem has moved me deeply
and the book has fallen onto my lap –
I look through the window
at the falling leaves the winds are stripping
from the trees which are now nearly bare –
long gone the cherry blossoms and the elder flower ...
it's over for now, but do not despair
leaves will be green again
and he who has gone
and taken your heart
will come back

So come, wipe away your tears!
the winds have been taking the prayers
you've uttered in the evenings at the window
to where you've hoped they would go.

MY SECRET ME

My secret me
hidden from eyes of all but mine
my unguessed-at other
unlike that which I weave and spin
the one I make for you to see
that struts about and plays the part
of someone you might think better
than the one that lurks behind you cannot see
who evades the harder tasks upon his path

This is the one which will not die
and which to myself I know as I
that will go through death to the other side
of the side that you can see

Once there it will wander aimless, disembodied
too unresolved and heavy still to fly on onwards
a flitting, awkward form of little substance
save for the shadows of what it left unfinished –
and so will seek another womb to bring it back
to do what before it had gone there to do.

BLOSSOMS ON THE CHERRY TREE

The girl, sleek black hair
and pink complexion blossoms
on the cherry tree.

AND I THOUGHT AND I TURNED AND I THOUGHT

I came home in the cold and the snow
and felt I'd got nowhere to go
the night was very crisp and very clear
and my heart was very cold

I stayed up until in the dying stars' light
I laid my head on the pillow by yours
and I lay awake in the pale light
and I thought and I turned and I thought

I looked at you and was full of pain
was I really going to leave you
and dash all your hopes again?

AVEC SON MEC MARIE...

The village band strikes up an air
one two three
one two three
and on the green Marie
is dancing not with me
one two three
one two three
she's dancing with her mec
under the linden tree
un deux trois
un deux trois
avec son mec
dans ses bras
avec moi
elle ne danse pas...

THE WANDERER SAYS GOODBYE TO HIS COAT

Farewell coat! I'm leaving here and I can't take you with me
you hang on the peg by the door
where you've always hung here in Budapest
ready for me to slip into on cold winter mornings
you've always been there for me and now
I'm going to abandon you
like a poor dog
and you don't know it yet

I bought you in Istanbul
all those years ago
and felt so snug inside you
that cold day with winter creeping up
and about to envelop the city with mists and fog
which made the Bosphorous vanish
and hands in your warm pockets
collar turned up I strode along the twisting streets
and to the heights along the ancient walls
where cutting winds dashed about like knives
and I was so glad of you
and whirling like a Dervish in you my swirling cloak
we did a scarecrow dance and chased away the crows of
   sorrows.

IT SLOWLY DAWNS ON ME

Morning crept through my window very gently
it began with the sound of a solitary bird
a thin plaintive cry over the meadows
mingling with my dream at first, as an emissary
sent to fetch me out of sleep
and, as along a woodland path which opens out onto sunlit
　　fields,
I awoke, the first light inching into the room
and expanding, moving into corners
and dissolving shadows
and casting others

A dog in the village barks
once, twice and then is quiet
thoughts come back, drifting through my mind
as clouds are doing outside across the sky –
they trouble me and I ask myself why
in the letter I got just yes-
terday you'd written as you had

As though in that last, fevered, embrace just before I'd left
you hadn't whispered in my ear 'I'll always love you, come
　　what may' –
and then in the letter you say 'I hope you'll be happy in love,
good luck
don't dream!'

And I really don't get what you mean.

ANNETTE...

This was more than I could ever have dreamt
to be sitting alone under a tree
with Annette

Though she was to wed the very next day
I stretched out my hand to her hand
which was lying in her lap

She was upset and ran away
and never again did I sit
under a tree with Annette...

I KNEW A POET IN ROMANIA

I knew a poet in Romania
I kissed her once
in the snow falling round us

She was wise enough to know
it couldn't last
and drove away quickly
while she still could

In the night a warm wind
came up from the south
and melted the snow
where we had stood.

SHE

She's a little bit clumsy and sometimes gauche
if there's a cup or a plate or a vase
to be knocked from a table
it's her that will do it
and if someone laughs at an inappropriate moment
it'll be her

She soaks up Mozart like a sponge –
you see she's really very musical
and I always sit beside her when I can
to catch a little tune she might be humming
or a sudden squeal which makes me jump
out of my skin, it's that
of many things
I love about her

And as for poetry, in that she delights
as though she were the very maker of that realm
which with a wand she summons up
a world from which she takes
the stuff of all the poems she writes down in a book

And just as when a conductor
with a twitch of his baton sets in motion
the voices of a choir
I have heard the heavenly music
locked in the trees and the stones and the stars
released by her with a wave of her hand –

She
mistress of sudden, unsuspected things!

And a thing that really intrigues me
is the things she finds so funny where others don't –
the kind of things that, lying under a willow tree
on a summer's noon when all is hushed
and drifting off might come to you
brought on the breeze by a man with a funny accent
in a frock-coat and a Hungarian hat
who trips over the phrase 'by your leave' or 'at your behest'
and leaves you a boxful of jumbled up dreams
that end before they begin and begin after they end...
yes, it's at things like these she'll crack her sides
things that others wouldn't find funny
 just very odd

But then *she* wouldn't laugh at the things that they would
she'd find them silly
and they would perplex her.

WEATHER VANE

I swing
according to the wind
I'm a proud copper cockerel and my home's this church
perched on top of the tower

I look down on the slate and tile of the village rooftops
over the meadows and fields
and I can see as far as the eye can see
all over Salisbury Plain

How I adore the seasons, especially the spring!
when soft breezes full of the scents
of the awakening earth and the elder flower
caress my face and ruffle my plumage
with its new flaming feathers which dazzle

I crow with the cocks of the farmyards at dawn
with a clarion call from my metal beak
and from my vantage point up here
I'm the first to herald the new-born disc
rising in the east
back from its journey through the abyss

Clouds drift silently over me
changing their shapes into pretty hens
who flutter down and dance before me
I the ruler of the roost!

Scores and scores of years I've been up here
witnessing the turning of the years

the seasons and the celebrations when the bells ring out
in ecstatic peals which boom in the belfry below me
and out across the rooftops and the fields

I see the storks bring souls for birth
in through windows where a light's been burning
all through the night –
I hear the cry of anguish
and the cry of delight

I see them grow, the generations –
pushed in their prams, play by the brook,
go with their satchels to school
walk with their sweethearts in the lanes
start a family of their own
go to work, go to war, some not return

Many's the tear I've shed
at the sad processions of funerals
when a lone bell tolls and a coffin's borne
to a hole which awaits it in the earth –
it might seem strange but I'm interwoven with their lives
and I share their grief and I share their joys

I have an eye
in case you've been wondering how I can cry
you can see right through it
to the sky on the other side

My greatest friends are the winds
they come from all directions

some of them of inestimable length
travelling for days on end with many miles still to go
who bring me news from far and wide
as do couriers to kings
I know what's in store in these rumours of war
and the gathering clouds in foreign lands
soon I'll see the men in khaki
hear the roll of a drum and a trumpet call
as women in tears line the high street
I've seen it all before

Others are local winds
that come up from the valley or down from the hills
they're the playful ones with whom I frolic
who spin me on my stand
and whisper things in my listening ear

I know misses so and so's having an affair
and so soon after her wedding day
I know why the farmer shot himself
and why there's a blight on the crops this year

I am here on high
looking down
sometimes swinging round.

I CANNOT EXTRACT FROM THESE SORROWS THE PLOUGH

You've become a kind of shadow
of what once you were
pale and thin and bags beneath your eyes –
your former glory's faded
it saddens me to see...
though trails of lipstick pursue me still through dreams
where scarlet as ever's the flesh between your thighs

And when I ask you why
you have thus become
you sigh:

'It is your smile
which fades when you see me
that causes leaves to fall

I have listened long for the lute
to pluck a chord
which will not diminish beyond my hearing
as hope has done beyond my hoping

And I cannot extract from these sorrows the plough
which puts these furrows in my brow'.

AFFAIR

Green blanket hung
over the balcony – all clear
up in the lift, fifth floor

Eye in the spy hole – quick look
opens a crack, slip in

Jacket flung over the back of a chair
skirt and trousers on the floor
phone off hook

In love and war
all's fair.

CHANNEL CROSSING

Lights along the lines
headlong into darkness
to where your love was waiting –
or was it?

Arrival Gare du Nord
cold November dawn
clutch receiver in my hand
phone ringing by your bedside
keeps on ringing.

YOU CANNOT QUITE CATCH HER EYE

Last days of August and summer soon will die
just a little more to hang on to
but it's all but gone, all but over
and you sigh

As when you hold her
in the madness of the station
her clasp not quite what it used to be
and you know the best is over
as she keeps glancing over her shoulder
and you cannot quite catch her eye.

ONLY THE DEVIL KNEW

I drank some wine – a lot!
I crawled around on the floor
and clawed at the carpet
I waited and waited for your call
which came not –
Where were you?

Only the devil knew –
I did not!

THESE POEMS WHICH FESTER IN THE DARKNESS

I don't like writing these poems
these poems which fester in the darkness
they hang upside down like bats in a dark place
and fly out in the daytime as well as the night
which is not in the natural order of things

They shout and scream on the page
are full of pity, pity me!
aggrieved, wronged
and seething with rage

They are not poems
they are rants from a dark place
scratched into brittle sheaves of paper
with a jagged nib and blooded ink –
it is quite natural she should leave

I look down at my wrist –
O *god*!

FULL YOUTH AND BLEEDING

It was in Paris
full youth and bleeding
the stage set
we met

Then on a pillow
wet with sweat
my head was laid
my wrist was slit

I CAN CHANGE THE FORTUNES OF MEN

I'm a rough formation
hewn by the elements and time
my age you cannot imagine
nor any amount of memory fathom

I was invoked and I made this rock my home
my spirit pervades this craggy crest
though they that invoked me are long gone

It pleases me here so I remain
I delight in the winds
and the rain bathes my blue-grey lichen-covered skin
and I can face in all directions at once
as could they who called me up –
for men were like that then

I know the courses of all the stars
and see the lines which join them up
into the shapes of the beings they are
and I delight to see them dance
round and round the ribbon
wound around the world

I can conduct thunder storms from here
which shake the earth and have the sea
rise up over the land and land
to emerge from the sea –
many's the island I've conjured up
out of the depths
in this manner

I can whip the waves to sudden rage
and have the sturdiest ships go under –
likewise the winds' directions I can change
and thereby alter the course a ship is on
so that it reaches the fabled lands beyond the rim
of solid earth which is left behind

Or I can turn a man inward on his quest
to navigate that inner sea beyond the mind
and attain the thing most precious in its depths

Thus can I change the fortunes of men
turn them in their course and make things happen
which otherwise wouldn't.

NOW IT'S SPRING, LOOK AROUND!

Allow the things of themselves
to reveal their meaning
listen to the birds
they sing not for nothing

allow these things to seed
something in the soil of your soul
and let it grow

now it's spring
look around
things are pushing from the ground!

SHE WINKS HER EYE AT HIS CONUNDRUM

With eyes
slightly askance
and seeing not single
and the stars themselves
somewhat out of kilter

the poet
regards his glass of wine

half empty
half full?
he cannot tell

He squints at the moon
one hand over an eye –
is she one, is she two
is she empty, is she full
or somewhere in between?
half empty
half full?
this he cannot either tell

Amused at his conundrum
she winks her eye
and begins to swell

Till full in the sky
she does to his wine
what she does to the tides

And lo and behold his vessel's full!

I IMAGINE LI PO

I imagine Li Po would have halted
at many a wayside inn such as this
and in his note book written
of a serving girl like Tâm
who at the moment's playing
havoc with my senses and my heart

And I reckon like me he'd be drinking
a veritable river of wine
as endless as the river of stars
to which he'd most likely be singing –
and from time to time he'd no doubt cast
in her direction a longing glance

And I bet he'd be as dismayed as me
when each time he looked
she looked away –

But that's perhaps the way she plays it
the game of love which I suspect's her art –
and as Li Po would know
it's not meant to be easy
to catch a girl's heart!

I CLOTHE THIS SKELETON

It's dark outside and over my desk
I hold my skull in my hands
my fingers in the sockets of my eyes
which are hollows and can no longer cry

As the bones inside my fingers hold the pen
which scrapes across the page I become aware
that I clothe this skeleton which has grown inside me
and been my frame and held me upright on the earth
and will, as I advance in years and shrink,
stretch my skin like ancient parchment
like the canvas of an artist stretched on its frame

And though it too will age and start to creak
as the marrow in it ebbs away,
becoming drier as it moves towards the dust
it will become some distant day,
it will long outlast me in this world –
abandoned, cast off, forgotten in its grave
forsaken by the flesh it once supported
which will have putrified
and I who will have transmigrated.

AT THE TIME OF THE BLOOD

She with the wild and tangled hair
with her lash and scorn and withering stare
has cast me in stone up here
mute and petrified
to join the company of the damned and dead
on this jagged crest of barren rock
for something said which was not wise
at the time of the blood
which ordained these things

O menses!
the nothing which is nothing
the empty moon
and the battering sea in my veins
are all that remain –
and Medusa
with her shriek and wound.

MISS MERVÉ

Miss Mervé, keep beguiling me
you cannot imagine how much I like it!
when you sit at your desk and you ask:
'Sir, is love a verb or a noun?'
challenging, your eyes flashing – what can I say
unstoppably – in front of the others
who have already noticed – that love is an active verb
it can also be a noun
but never passive – (and you don't give me much sleep!)
... 'but,' you argue,'it surely can be passive, as in 'to be loved'

O, I know! you full well know (you flummox me!)
you're loved by me, Miss Mervé!

MY ARITHMETIC'S NOT QUITE UP TO THAT

Oh how I love a lunchtime session
when all the birds are tweeting in heaven
and in the fields they're making hay
as today this merry May, with two times ten already drunk
and one for the road makes three times seven
and add to that one more than that
and it's twenty two pints all told –
or so I'm told...
for in my befuddled state here on the floor
my arithmetic's not quite up to that.

ÖZGÜR

It's no use my pretending
I'm not lost when you look at me
your almond eyes when you came to earth
were put there to beguile such fools as me

Nor am I very grateful to God
that he made you so many years after me
for had it been otherwise
it might not be beyond the realm of hope
when you look at me

But Özgür, alas, we must remain
as far apart in love as we are in age.

PHILIP THE BALD

His portrait hangs somewhere or other
possibly in Krakow up at the palace
he looks frightfully important
and liked to be known as Philip the Bold

I forget which nation he's supposed to have ruled
but I do remember that he was bald
not at all bold as he'd like you to think, but bald
and that was how he earned his title
the one all his subjects knew him by
Philip the Bald

And because he kept his bonce well shined
all the lights of the city, whichever city it was,
were reflected in his polished pate
as was the moon and all the stars
just like an astrolabe

But that was only late at night
when no one about he'd take off his hat
his feathered hat which made him look
much alike to a cockatoo.

ADVICE TO THE YOUTH WHICH ONCE WAS I

Are you to remain just talking
now that the wine bottle's empty
and the candle's burnt low?...
or are you going to take things further
which would be the obvious thing to do
had you the confidence and you knew

... what it means
when she lowers her eyes and twines her hair
falling silent, as if preoccupied, and a million miles from you...
then suddenly looking up throws a challenging look
to which you cannot rise and you drop your eyes –
the last thing you should do!

Get over the fear she might protest
if you lean over and at last you kiss her –
better by far to fear the wretched cock who heralds dawn
whose pallid fingers will steal round the curtains
turning this magic night to hum-drum day –
and to realise before it's too late
that the thing for which you've been so ardently longing
is what she's waiting for!

STORM IN THE HARBOUR

The fishing boats
huddled like sheep in their fold
creak in their moorings
and jostle one another

The eucalyptus trees bent double
are flayed by the wind and a lone crow
turns somersaults in the sky

The awnings of the cafés are rolled back
and their doors are tightly shut
as the waves rush upon the harbour wall
and drench the glistening road that runs along the front

I hurry to my lodgings
my umbrella turned inside out.

PATMOS

The island is criss-crossed with dry stone walls
built by strong weather-beaten hands
wedged in and fitted stone by stone
that no kind of weather nor clambering goat nor time
can unloose
and they hold the island together
with orchards of olives and vines –

A sad old donkey in his paddock brays
a fishing boat puts out to sea
with wheeling sea-gulls in its wake
flat-roofed houses square and white
higgle-di-piggledy climb the hill
crowned on its crest by the monastery
whose bells tinkle and chime and boom
across the bay.

ENGÜR

Engür – what does her name rhyme with?
I can't think as she writes in her book
her scent is overpowering my capacity
to think any thought beyond:
I think you're magnificent in every conceivable way
your sleek black hair and your painted nails
clenched around your pen...
your eyes transfix me when you look up
asking me if what you've written is good
English – 'It is I assure you!' though really it isn't
but I've lost the ability to in any way
displease her and I ask her to read it out
for just to hear her accent makes my heart melt
and I'm lost – her name rhymes with lure...

LOST IN THE SHADOWS I'VE THROWN AROUND MY SOUL

I am not who I am
and this disquiets me
and I wander and I search for a remedy –
I am sad and far from home
and as far from myself as I'll ever be
myself my enemy
in clothing ragged and torn

I've ripped the clothing off my back
I move amongst the pine trees and am alone –
poised between the ragged cliffs
and a dark ravine
must I go on?

One step to the left and one to the right
where is the mitigating factor
in I this reckless actor

I who am not who I am...
who's this I that does not know
and where's that one that might?

It's lost in the shadows I've thrown around my soul.

THE PHOTOGRAPH

You're looking into my eyes –
for it's I that am taking the photograph –
sitting in the olive grove in the long grass
your hands are folded on one another
on your knee

Dropping down a little furtively
my eyes alight upon your thighs
clad in jean and run
along to where they meet –
at that ardently coveted
as yet unattained
part of your anatomy

Your eyes are apprehensive, anxious
and seem to be saying:
I know you want me there – all men do –
and it troubles me that you do too...
because I'm really very confused
and don't know whether I don't or whether I do.

THIS HAS MY HEART MOVED

This
has my heart moved
and prompted my tongue
to the telling of it

The tear
spilling from your eye
that you tried to hide
and your hand
you'd raised to wave goodbye
falling lifeless to your side.

AROUSAL

Her short black skirt rides
up her white thighs as she bends
to wipe red table.

IT WAS LONDON THAT YOU WANTED

I thought that as we'd met in April
and you'd in passing said you might
be coming down to the countryside
and if you did you'd look me up
which set me dreaming as dream I do
that the summer might be one of long country walks
of kissing in barns and making love
in fields of hay and shaded woods
and drinking beer in village pubs
in the long summer evenings
and swearing undying love –
all this and much much more
before September when apples fall

But autumn frosts have killed those thoughts –
you never did come down, or if you did,
you didn't look me up
and, as you've written in this letter, what I'd imagined
wasn't what you'd had in mind at all –
it was London that you'd always wanted
and all that that implied –
all that I abhor.

LEYLA

Leyla, you're so retiring, so shy – why?
you could conquer myriads of hearts
with your face, your eyes, your slender grace,
starting with mine!

In those rare moments when you look up
from your books and catch my eye
I swear I'm like a defeated army
that throws down its arms and puts up its hands
and resigns itself to captivity, if not death

Leyla, tell me, in your nearly perfect English
why you're so shy – is it a burning passion
in your breast, that by your downcast eyes
you try to repress?

AYSEGÜL

You shouldn't wear those stockings, young lady
those meshed webs of glistening gossamer
which run right up your thigh and higher...
they entangle me in their nylon tendrils like a fly –

Are you aware of the nature of the thoughts they arouse in me?
if I told you you'd blush...
You blush? you cool as a cucumber, white-skinned lynx – yes,
you'd blush with delight!

CURSED AM I

She leans in a doorway in just a negligée
she beckons to the men who strip her with their eyes –
a far sad cry from when she'd lean on her gate
in her village by the river
waiting for me

I broke her heart one day and then the city
swallowed her and made her tricky –
and cursed am I who pass unseen
and strip her of her negligée.

STRAYMUM

She's one of those beauties that abound in Phnom Penh
her mouth quick to smile and her hair a silky sheen
Li Po saw immortals and I saw Straymum

I'm incurably enraptured, I'm at my wits' end
she's leaning in the doorway and her eyes have strayed to me
and she lowers them and then she opens them
and then she lowers them again

And my heart's set adrift on the river
which flows to Can Tho.

TO AN UNKNOWN WOMAN PASSING

Because you'll never be known to me
further than my hungry eyes which follow you
as you traverse this sunlit square
towards the arches which will swallow you
in this town I'm passing through

I will light an eternal flame
in an alcove in my memory
and kneel before your flickering image
and put a golden diadem in your hair
to flash in the sun as you cross the square

And it might just be you'll reappear
– with the right libation and prayer –
the sunlight glinting in the diadem
as you head towards me across the square.

OUT OF MY MIND – OUT!

It's gone midnight
it's time to think about...no! I cannot sleep!
I shall pull on my boots and go walking
and let dawn find me shuddering
on a step down by the river –
or somewhere...I don't care

The sun's glinting on the Fontanka
I lean from the bridge of the horses
and try to stop my eyes from closing
and keep away from the flow of my thoughts
the things around which they rush and eddy
and try to treat the morning
as though it were the first morning of my life
my only morning
my mind a blank
not blighted by those things you said which crushed me
and have kept me walking around Saint Petersburg all night
out of my mind out of my mind – Out!

I wish I could mount the bronze horses on this bridge
and gallop to the sun
and be done with 'Love', this leaden thing!

WHEN I, WITH MANY THOUGHTS IN MIND

It happened when I
with many thoughts in mind
came upon a fox
crossing the path which leads up the hill –
she turned and looked me right in the eye
and then to my astonishment said:

'You know these woodland paths
like the back of your hand
but nothing like as well as I do –
your head's in the clouds, you think too much
and never do you sniff the air –
if you did perhaps you'd see
things you'd not expect to see,'
and she spoke in slanted rhyme
when her silver bark turned to a human tongue

I mused upon the vixen's words and sniffed the wind
in just the way she'd shown me before she slinked away –
and all of a sudden another world appeared
one long-buried beneath all my thinking
as though the essence of everything around emerged
shining, full of subtle scents, raw sensations, intuitions
and unseen shapes both far and near
fashioned from the short sharp sips of air
which flicked on a current long-disconnected

And in long-forgotten flashes of clarity
in a mind unencumbered with its usual debris
of things past and future which ceased to exist

as though I'd stepped out of a confining shell
all manner of beings both strange and familiar
took on form as they emerged from a mist
previously hidden, now in plain sight

And that night lying awake I heard the shrill baying of a fox
up on the hill amongst the silver trees beneath the moon
and I wondered whether it was her and what she was telling –
I sniffed the breeze which bathed my face
coming in through the window
on that warm mid-summer's night
and lo and behold there she was, my vixen,
sat upon her haunches
midst a troupe of dancers spinning round
all in coloured caps and gowns!

THREE POEMS TO AUTUMN

1

It is the time when
I take long walks in the hills
gathering what remains in the hedgerows

Blackberries long gone
and the berries on the elder
have been pecked away –
their pale leaves cling and twirl
and are fewer and thinner each time I pass this way

Starlings flock in dark whirling clouds
which disappear southward
over the plain.

2

I used to come here in the blood-hot summer
to this clearing in the trees and strip
and play with my imaginary nymph
O maniacs! and now I huddle in a greatcoat
under this great whispering pine
collar pulled up against the cold.

3

Mushrooms push up from the dank earth
I lie on my stomach and breathe
vapours from the underworld
where Persephone went
and from which with spring flowers
she'll return to us.

HOMESICKNESS

I like this Russian winter we're having
the snow lies thick on the ground
and crunches under my boots
as I walk beneath the silver birch

But I feel a little glum this evening
my thoughts and heart keep drifting
like the snow on this Arctic wind
to my home, the rambling old house
back in my village on the edge of the Plain
where my mother (ageing now, I fear dread news any day)
moves about in her dreams
and the barking dogs running to greet me
as I come with my rucksack up the drive.

WRECKED ON THE BALTIC

Up on the deck we're soaked by the spray
and we bellow our songs to the roar of the wind
whilst the engines sputter and throb down below

We'd set our course on a distant star
which now we've lost sight of in the blackened sky
and in its place loom cliffs and crags
where monsters lurk and Sirens perch
poised to madden our minds with their unearthly singing
(as though we'd not been maddened enough by earthly
   women!)
and then to devour our souls
to waste them away with longing

The furious wind batters against our bows
the mast near to breaking and the sails in shreds
the steering shaft buckled and the deck awash
and down below it's filling with water
as we roll from starboard to port
the towering waves like fortress walls
with hissing foaming crests along their turrets
and astern our wake's like the wake of the dead

Captain Tim, I cried
this could be the end of us...
we could be heading down to Hades,
to Davey Jones' Locker

We could indeed, said he
so let us drain this bottle
lest we arrive there sober!

TIPSY ON THE TURVY GREEN

Elderflower-scented, the breeze
rustles the fresh green leaves
we are wine-high
in the Hungarian spring

Csárdás have us spin
tipsy on the turvy green
girls swirl, show thigh –
open your petals
let me in!

WINTER WALKS ALONG THE DANUBE

Winter walks along the Danube
late afternoon, lights of Budapest in the distance
barges – great black hulks – looming out of the mist
and under the bridges
your hand in mine – you, new in my life
breathing summer fire into my mouth
in your black coat and black hat
and that huge wounded heart
that was singing again

Let's buy some wine, you said
and go home and light the candles!

WITH SOMETHING AKIN TO HOPE

There were times when I would be
just the same as her, silent and moody and then
getting drunk go out and disappear –
and I remember the pain
of she who'd waited up
in vain
and how it usually ended in the end

The night is getting on and the moon has set
I stare from the window over the city
she's out there somewhere
and she won't be coming back –
not tonight
what's left of it...

And in the morning, if she does
she won't say a word of where
nor with whom
she's been –
and I won't want to know

Nevertheless I listen
with something akin to hope
for footsteps on the stairs.

SHE COMES TO PICK UP HER THINGS

The lights were on in my flat
it was her of course, she still had the key
and we hugged as I walked through the door
just like old times
which made it doubly sad

She went through the cupboards
and through the drawers
of her one-time home

A dress and some stockings
some books and some Chinese plates
and some other little parts of herself
I blinked back a tear

Wrap up warm, I said, the night is cold
and I pulled her winter hat down
over her ears as she left.

I CANNOT GO IN!

Coming back from work, the tram crowded
outside darkness fallen early
mist and lights on the river as we cross Margit Bridge
the comforting sound of the voice announcing the stops
I relish every moment more I can sit here
gazing out of the window, no particular thoughts
just a drifting of vague things which stifle the heart's scream
until the terminal at Moscow Square
where I must get off and go home –
in front of my door I freeze
it's empty inside –
I cannot go in!

MY POEM

And we walked off in different directions
there were no words, a silent reproach said it all

The sun was beginning to slope down the sky
into a cold horizon with winter creeping up

I followed you with my eyes for a while
and then they dropped back into the pavement
I knew where you were going

Forgive me if my poem reaches out to grab you back
it has a life of its own, I have merely released it

It follows you to where you are going
I just drop my eyes onto the pavement and am sad

But my poem follows you along the street
it is ready to do violence, to grab you and force you to the
    ground
and to stop you going where you're going

My poem rides the winds
it soars above the mountain tops
it fecundates the stars!

My poem is a thousand feet tall
it was written in a bottle of wine
over the course of an evening

washed down with a full moon
and it rides on the surge of an orgasm –
this is what it is

The pavement is flat and I trudge along it
my hands in my pockets
thinking back to what once was
and now is not
and it leads down into the metro
and we're heading in different directions

But my poem is rushing about like the demon it is
up to the stars and grabbing at you
it is laughing crying leaping fucking
an uncontrollable force which is thrusting itself out of me
I who am lost

Now it's breaking windows, kicking in doors –
it wants you back!

THE TIME HAS COME I THINK

We sleep together
yet sleep apart
back to back
not heart to heart
the time has come I think
to part.

THAT IS WHY I AVERT MY EYE

I look in the mirror and I see myself
but is it myself that I see
and does the other looking back
think that I'm a counterfeit
and not what I think myself to be?

I cannot look for long
into those other eyes that stare
out of the surface of the glass
I have to drop my gaze

For they seem to have their roots
in a deeper earth, a darker world
and much more old than I
they mock and they accuse –
and that is why I avert my eye.

CHANTRAI

I could dally here the whole day long
as long as there's this girl to flirt with
who's already since I've been here drinking
lassooed my heart with her eyes and her whimsy

Her name she tells me is Chantrai
and this is the seventh jug she's brought me
here by the river in Phnom Penh

The hours are passing very quickly
each one filled with Chantrai's glances
and each one wished to never end
filled with joy my sad heart dances

I'd mount her on my dashing stallion
and round the heavens in a frenzy gallop
if another jug of wine were to come my way

But alas at close of day
my money's spent and I must away!

WAKING AWAY FROM A DREAM

But who is...was she?
and why have we been wrenched from that embrace
and how
can I ever find her again... ever...ever
in this labyrinth of alleys
in this unknown, yet strangely remembered town
with doors with no numbers
numerous and nameless as the stars
through one of which she's slipped –
and they are all now disappearing...
and waking away from the dream
clutching at fragments of mind
which break off
I'm washed ashore –
whilst the dream drifts away.

SAPPHO

I love the poems you have written!
tell me once again
about your life in Mytilene
the little white town on that windswept isle –
for in your telling you take me back
and conjure up again
the magic enchantment of my youth

I walked out with you on a translucent morning
the smell of the pine trees and the wild thyme
borne on the light wind off the sea
and I asked you how they came to you your poems
and you said it was as though
a little bird dropped them out of the air –
at that you started singing
and a shiver ran up my spine
'a delicate flame which ran beneath my skin'
and quickened a seed in me
which had lain in the earth in the dark
which then I nurtured till it started to grow
and ever since I've tended
like a precious vine which
– just as you told me –
needs joy and sorrow and pain
sunshine and rain you said,
as for anything if it's to grow

And that's what made me
turn my hand to song
with what you sowed in me
all those many years ago.

I WAS A YOUTH AND SADLY WANTING

It was in a wayside tavern in the Tyrol
I sat drinking a draught of beer and smoking my pipe
whilst the waitress in an apron with lovely flaxen hair
moved from table to table with the grace of a sprite –
and every now and then she glanced my way
seeming with a question in her look
but panic-stricken, tongue-tied, knotted-up inside
I dropped my eyes –
for I was a youth and sadly wanting
in such things as these

And I wondered on my way home,
pausing on the bridge over the rushing river
– torrid as the longings tormenting my soul –
how she'd take the little note I'd slipped
under the beer mat and whether
on the morrow I should go back
a little bolder and see –
or just be inept, leave it at that
sling my rucksack over my shoulder
and be on my way.

THE REST IS A BLUR OF CRIMSON AND BLACK

One evening, when the moon was dangling in the sky
in her first quarter crescent, sharp as a scythe, I
went down to the harbour where I'd heard
the sound of a lyra amplified over the town
its daemonic strings calling out to my blood
already stirring in these first days of spring

It was up one of those twisting alleys
that lead off from the harbour of Hania, I saw her
through the steamed up window of a taverna –
she was set apart from all around her
sitting alone at the bar in a tight-fitting bodice
with sleek, black, hair down to her shoulder –
the very goddess, it seemed, of love and desire…
I hesitated a moment, for some deep foreboding
told me not to proceed –
but my blood was not to be cheated
and she swiveled on her stool
as I walked through the door

I sat at a table and ordered some wine
the place was crowded, mainly with men
and I cautioned myself to be careful, remembering
a similar place where one such as she
was casting her nets and maddening
the minds of men such as these –
(all I'd done was to buy her a drink
and in a pool of blood I'd ended up
outside on the street)

But now as I sat at this chequered table
a glass in my hand which emptied and filled
emptied and filled
she fixed her eyes upon me
under lowered lashes through the smoke
as though I were her prey, she kept them on me
kept them on me
until at last
myself now maddened with the music and the drink
I cast all caution to the wind and for one brief ecstatic
    moment
my face was buried in her breast –

And the rest is a blur of crimson and black
for what was to follow happened so quick.

GINA

Well-serious is she, with little humour
but pretty as a wren, with hair to her shoulder –
a studious maid not given to pleasure
or so she would say, but I'd be prepared to wager

A little wine would undo her demeanour
and she'd sidle up close and begin to titter
whilst my stealthy hand would seek out her treasure
and all would be well in bed with Gina.

THE COIN

I saw you come in the door
one of those doors with a tinkling bell
common to antiquarian shops
and I wanted to tell you my story
and so I got you
to come over and pick me up
which was not difficult to do
for being made of Venus's own pure metal
I have certain powers of attraction

I'm not worth much to people these days
for I'm but a one kopek copper coin
from eighteen something and something
you see, the last numbers have worn away
and I myself am not sure
of just exactly when I was born

But the womb I sprang from was in Cyprus
from deep underground and my mother as I said
was Venus, Aphrodite if you like
and still unformed I was taken to Moscow
and there I went through fire
and was hammered on a forge
until I was a round bright shining disc
like my mother
who shines as the Morning and the Evening Star –
and then my worth was great
and I was handed from hand to hand
O, how hands delighted to hold me
a new-minted copper kopek!

There's not the effigy of the Czar on my face
just the imperial crown and emblem of Russia
around which vast land I would travel
from village to village, from town to town
in uncountable people's pockets
and exchanged for bread, for beer, for vodka, tobacco
I went from high places to low
from the fine houses of the gentry
to the hovels of the peasants
and to the brothels and the markets and the inns
and many's the time I heard the words 'heads or tails?'
as I was spun in the air in a wager

So you see, I was always circulating, always in use
except when I was being kept, with others of my kind
in a box, in a warm kitchen perhaps, by someone saving up
for a horse or a plough or a wedding ring –
and those were blessed times, as when a horse
is put out to rest in a field of clover

You see, I was highly valued then
but in time my power diminished
and then the Revolution came
and everything changed for the worst
and I was replaced by inferior alloys
and was tossed away as something worthless

But now you have found me and heard my tale
take me home and I will prove to be of great value –
my mother is the goddess of attraction
and I can attract to you
something of much more value than money
or all the gold in the world could ever buy.

Nets in the Wind

YOU'D PUT ON YOUR SHOES THE WRONG WAY ROUND

It began to register
there might be someone other
by the time the penny'd dropped
here you already were not

You'd put on your shoes
the wrong way round
so that I'd follow you
the wrong way
round
you decoyed me
over to where you weren't –
like a plover with its cry of 'peewit' –
with letters postmarked Paris and Moscow
where now I know you were neither

Thrown off the scent I went round and round
in circles ever widening I went
like a hound in pursuit of a hare –
to here and there and otherwhere
and all your zig-zag zigging
with your footprints in reverse
led me back to here
where only myself I find

I may as well fling
my nets in the winds
in the hope of catching the sky
as any chance of catching you –
duplicitous tricky transparent thing!

WHERE HAVE YOU GONE?

You're not on the lawns where the mazes are
I've searched through all their twists and turns
and I've just got giddy from going round and square

And you're not in the orchard where I thought you might
be hiding in an apple, a plum or a pear
nor down at the lake where sometimes you walk
singing your songs which I delight to hear

And I don't see your shadow in the face of the dial
which marks off the hours as the sun revolves –
nor in the riddle do you seem to be hidden
engraved in the stone which covers the well
and whose answer depends on whoever you are

And try as I might I cannot espy you
in the tapestry which hangs in the hall
where knights and ladies sometimes ride
before they return to a time unknown

I've searched in the mirror where sometimes I catch
out of the corner of my eye
sight of things as they flit to and fro
but nothing I've seen apart from my face

Down in the cellars I've opened the barrels
but only fermentation's happening inside –
and in the retort where the spirit's distilled
I've gazed in vain for your shape to appear

On the verge of despair an inner voice tells me
I'm not likely to find you anywhere here...
you may have returned to where you came from
and if I turn my gaze inward I'll find you in there.

THE RIVER OF TIME WHICH NEVER RETURNS

As a worker in wood
might cast his eye around his workshop
for off-cuts over the years he's discarded
I look through my notebooks
for things I have scribbled
up on the hills, in a train, or a pub
a fragment, a phrase or some reflection
on which I'd closed the book and forgotten –
but coming upon again I turn it around in my mind
as the woodworker would in his hand
and hum and ha and begin to envision

Perhaps it will fit with some other fragments
which have a similar feel and hue
and the grain flows in the same direction

Or perhaps it's enough to go off on its own
gathering words and phrases to it as it goes
creating a structure, building a body
and a heartbeat, a rhythm
to drive it onwards in what it wants to say

Or it may be some raw emotion
which clamours to cry its rage and its pain
and needs not ink but tears and blood
to scratch its fury onto the page

Or a simple observation of a stone or a tree
which needs but a word or two
simply to conjure it into the mind
and then to be left unhewn

And it may be
as I flick through one of these abandoned books
I come upon a flower pressed between its pages
given by you to me one long-ago summer
which brings it all back

As our sculptor in wood might sigh
coming upon a figure cut from willow
at the memory of a morning one May
as he sat with his sweetheart on the bank of a river
everything fresh and green and young as they
in the river of time which never returns.

Nets in the Wind

I TOOK HER WORDS TO MEAN WHAT SHE MEANT

Words are not what the heart works with
though they can throw it off the scent
and corral it into dismal corners
and cut it up with bloody blades

I took her words to mean what she meant
so they would all but kill me –
for it seemed they said how she really felt
and nothing I could do nor say could change it
written as they were in the stone of her heart
and under the lash of her whip was I

Her words she used as weapons
poisonous barbed arrows dipped in the venom
of cruel insinuations and things she knew would hurt
which when it pleased her she'd unleash from off her tongue
cutting me to the very quick
and making of me a saddened slave

She'd fashion lies from them too
– oh she was good at that! –
artfully thought-out alibis which covered her tracks
so I'd not see the extent of her deceit
and so believe her little 'errands' and her 'assignations'
were all quite innocent

But by and by I began to suspect
when I detected certain discrepancies in what she told me
times and places didn't tally and certain people didn't exist
though others I realised did –
and then in an ambush I caught her out
when coming back late one night she started her lies
which were as clear to me as the truth
they were supposed to hide

From then on I ceased to take her words
as being anywhere near to what they implied
and I learnt to wait
for anything else she'd muster in her panic
which would further annul them.

HELÈNE...

With you it was I crossed the Seine
and yours was the heart I longed to attain
to which lay the bridge I could not go over
as we walked apart across the river
that night I'd like to forget, Helène...

HIS WAND'S ASTIR AS IT WAS BEFORE

His sisters have put him together again
look at him there this starry night
every limb's become a star
and his wand's astir as it was before!

And in just such a manner
the heavens have put
you and I, hand in hand
back together.

NIGHT IN ISTANBUL

Tamara, you lovely slender crescent moon!
It's all I can do not to clasp and put to my lips
your hand when it brushes mine
as we walk side by side in old Istanbul

Tell me, in your lovely Turkish tongue
anything you will and I will listen -
or walk in silence and the falling darkness
and the rising moon will speak
the words you're holding in your tongue

Or simply give to me your hand
with its slender velvet fingers
tapering like the minarets of Sultan Ahmet
and it will be enough – for now at least -
though I may press for more
ere the sun comes up in the east.

GOT YOUR LETTER, FEEL BETTER!

The evenings are long
full of birdsong
I've seen your face in every place
where once I kissed it –
how I've missed it!

Wondered how you fared
if you still cared
whether another
had taken my place.

Got your letter
feel better!

www.ingramcontent.com/pod-product-compliance
Lightning Source LLC
Chambersburg PA
CBHW020124130526
44591CB00032B/522